Title: Red Kangaroo
R.L.: 1.0
PTS: 0.5
TST: 74745

Animals of the World

Red Kangaroo

By Edana Eckart

Children's Press®
A Division of Scholastic Inc.
New York / Toronto / London / Auckland / Sydney
Mexico City / New Delhi / Hong Kong
Danbury, Connecticut

Photo Credits: Cover, pp. 11, 21 (top right) © Gerard Lacz/Animals Animals; pp. 5, 21 (top left) © Mark Chappell/Animals Animals; pp. 7, 13, 21 (bottom left) © Tom Brakefield/Corbis; pp. 9, 17 © Steven David Miller/Animals Animals; p. 15 © Fritz Prenzel/Animals Animals; pp. 19, 21 (bottom right) © David Fritts/Animals Animals
Contributing Editor: Jennifer Silate
Book Design: Mindy Liu

Library of Congress Cataloging-in-Publication Data

Eckart, Edana.
  Red kangaroo / by Edana Eckart.
  v. cm.—(Animals of the world)
  Includes index.
  Contents: Red kangaroos—Hopping—Joeys.
  ISBN 0-516-24304-7 (lib. bdg.)—ISBN 0-516-27896-7 (pbk.)
  1. Red kangaroo—Juvenile literature. [1. Red kangaroo. 2. Kangaroos.] I. Title. II. Series: Eckart, Edana. Animals of the world.

  QL737.M35E34 2003
  599.2'223—dc21

                                        2002156202

Contents

Red kangaroos live in grassy places.

Some red kangaroos have red fur.

Some have gray fur.

Red kangaroos eat grass.

Red kangaroos have strong back legs.

They use their legs to hop.

11

Mother red kangaroos have **pouches**.

Baby kangaroos live inside the pouches.

13

Red kangaroo babies are called **joeys**.

Joeys are very small when they are born.

15

Red kangaroos sleep a lot during the day.

They sleep to stay cool when it is hot.

Red kangaroos live
in groups.

Groups of red kangaroos
are called **mobs**.

19

Red kangaroos are wonderful animals.

21

New Words

joeys (**joh**-eez) baby kangaroos

mobs (**mahbz**) groups of kangaroos

pouches (**pouch**-ehz) furry pockets on top of
female kangaroos' stomachs that are used
to hold and carry young kangaroos

red kangaroos (**red** kang-guh-**rooz**) large
animals with two very strong back legs
for hopping

To Find Out More

Books
Life Cycle of a Kangaroo
by Lisa Trumbauer
Capstone Press

The Kangaroo
by Sabrina Crewe
Steck-Vaughn

Web Site
Creature World: Red Kangaroo
http://www.pbs.org/kratts/world/aust/kangaroo/index.html
Read interesting facts about the red kangaroo on this Web site.

Index

About the Author
Edana Eckart has written several children's books. She enjoys bike riding with her family.

Reading Consultants
Kris Flynn, Coordinator, Small School District Literacy, The San Diego County Office of Education

Shelly Forys, Certified Reading Recovery Specialist, W.J. Zahnow Elementary School, Waterloo, IL

Sue McAdams, Former President of the North Texas Reading Council of the IRA, and Early Literacy Consultant, Dallas, TX